MOVIES

COMMUNICATION
TODAY & TOMORROW

LIBRARY OF CONGRESS CATALOGING-IN-PUBLICATION DATA

Balcziak, Bill, 1962-
    Movies / by Bill Balcziak.
      p. cm. -- (Communication)
    Includes index.
    Summary: Traces the history of motion pictures, explains how a film is financed, cast, shot, edited, released, and promoted, and describes the work of producers, directors, and other personnel involved in the making of a film.
    ISBN 0-86592-058-3
    1. Motion pictures--History--Juvenile literature. [1. Motion pictures--History.]
I. Title. II. Series: Communication (Vero Beach, Fla.)
PN1993.5.A1B27 1989
791.43'09--dc20
                                       89-33249
                                          CIP
                                       AC MN

MOVIES

TEXT BY
BILL BALCZIAK

DESIGN & PRODUCTION BY
MARK E. AHLSTROM
(The Bookworks)

**ROURKE
ENTERPRISES,
INC.**
Vero Beach, FL 32964
U.S.A.

MOVIES

TABLE OF CONTENTS

CREDITS

ILLUSTRATIONS:

Tom Carroll/FPG .... cover photo, 4

AP/Wide World Photos 7, 38, 45

The Bettmann Archive 9, 11, 13,
.... 16, 17, 20, 23, 24, 25, 27, 33, 40,

Leibowitz/FPG 19

Henry Gris/FPG 30

FPG 32, 34, 44

Nancy Ney/ FPG 36

L & M Photo/FPG 37

Lee Foster/FPG 39

Tom Tracy/FPG 43

J. Leung/FPG 44

TYPESETTING AND LAYOUT: THE FINAL WORD
PRINTING: WORZALLA PUBLISHING CO.

INTRODUCTION

The theater darkens. People hurry to put on the special glasses they were given at the door. There is a buzz of excitement as showtime grows near.

The audience quickly falls silent as a huge curtain begins to open. Without warning, a small brown object appears on the screen in front of the audience.

The object slowly grows larger and begins to move out into the audience! As it gets closer, the mysterious thing appears to be a moon or a planet. Hands reach out to hold the small, spinning globe. Nervous laughter erupts as people grab nothing but air.

Deep, pulsing music begins to swell. Suddenly, the scene shifts to the inside of a futuristic spaceship. Blinding laser beams streak across the theater. The sound of explosions rocks people in their seats. The spaceship is under attack!

Strange beings move around the spaceship. A small furry creature appears and seems to float right in front of the audience. And then, the moment everyone is waiting for: Captain EO—Michael Jackson—makes his appearance.

The audience cheers wildly as Captain EO barks out commands to his crew. The laser beams fade out. The audience sits back breathlessly. "How can this get any better?" they wonder.

It does.

Disney's magical 3D movie *Captain EO* hints at the future of motion pictures. It uses the latest sound and light technology—and lifelike 3D effects—to put the audience right in the middle of the action. If the inventors of moving pictures could see *Captain EO* they would be very impressed!

Movies like *Captain EO* are the very best kind of modern magic.

They make us want to return again and again to a fantasyland of sight and sound. That's why movies are so popular. They let us see things that are better than our dreams.

Ever since the early 1900's—when moving pictures were new and still rather clumsy—people have been flocking to movie theaters. More than $4.5 billion in movie tickcts wcrc sold in 1988! And the popularity of movies is growing every year.

This continuing success is due to many things. Some say that movies are getting better. Other claim that movies are one of the cheapest forms of entertainment these days. Whatever the reason, movies are here to stay.

Michael Jackson thrills audiences in Disney's magical 3D movie, Captain EO.

CHAPTER ONE

LIGHTS! CAMERA! ACTION!

It Started with 24 Horses

In 1873 an English photographer named Eadweard Muybridge set up 24 cameras in a long line along a race track near San Francisco. Attached to the shutter of each camera was a string, and inside was a small glass plate that was coated with light-sensitive chemicals. The string was then stretched across the track.

When everything was set up, Muybridge's assistant waited atop a horse at the starting line. Muybridge instructed his assistant to bring the horse to a steady gallop in front of the cameras near the finish line.

As the horse sped past Muybridge and the cameras, the strings were broken. This tripped the shutters. A series of photos was taken in a quick sequence. A slightly different image of the horse appeared on each plate after it was developed.

The 24 photos, when viewed as a set, gave Muybridge a clear image of how the horse galloped along the track. These photos, now famous, are considered the first "moving picture."

Muybridge used his technique to photograph other types of motion—including people walking and running. These pictures were published in books and later projected with a machine he called a zoöpraxiscope.

The projected images were not exactly "photographs." Using a special drawing set, Muybridge copied the original photos by hand onto glass plates. Then a bright light could be shined through the plates, which producing a rather fuzzy image on a screen or wall.

*This series of photos, simply called "Woman, Adjusting Train and Turning Around,"
was taken by Eadweard Muybridge in his search for a way to create moving pictures.*

Muybridge's experiments were very creative, but they never caught on with other photographers or the public. No one was excited about lugging 24 cameras around to capture motion on film.

Still, Muybridge's success was inspiring to men like Thomas Edison and Hannibal Goodwin of the United States, and the French brothers Auguste and Louis Lumière. Within a few years, each of these inventors had tried their hand at "filmmaking."

Goodwin on Film

Using Muybridge's process, a large glass plate was needed for each photograph. It had to be replaced with another plate to make another photo. Of course, only a single picture could be taken at a time. A series of cameras had to be set up to take multiple photos of a subject.

Hannibal Goodwin realized that taking pictures on one photographic plate at a time wasn't fast enough to show real motion. He developed a clear celluloid film base that would take the place of the clumsy glass plates.

Goodwin coated the plastic-like base with a light-sensitive coating, or film. The celluloid film could be moved quickly through a camera. This allowed a photographer to shoot a rapid series of pictures—or frames—with just a single camera.

Edison

In 1888 Thomas Edison—inventor of the phonograph—met Eadweard Muybridge. During their discussions about photography, Edison came up with ideas that really opened the door to filmmaking. He quickly contacted his assistant, William Dickson. Together they worked on putting Edison's ideas into practical form.

Dickson and Edison created two machines. One was used to photograph the subject. The other "played" moving pictures.

The first device was called the Kinetograph. It could take up to 40 photographs per second on celluloid film! Edison kept it in a specially

The Kinetoscope was invented by Thomas Edison in 1890. People watched moving pictures through a peephole at the top of the device.

built studio on the grounds of his laboratory. This studio, called the "Black Maria," was a large, black tar-paper shack with a roof that could be rolled back to let sunlight in.

Famous personalities such as Buffalo Bill and Annie Oakley were invited to the studio to perform for the new camera. After the performances were photographed and developed, they were projected inside a small cabinet called the Kinetoscope.

The boxlike Kinetoscope held about 50 feet of celluloid film— enough for hundreds of individual pictures. A glass peephole was placed on top of the device. By turning a crank and looking though the peephole, a person could see a moving picture of the performers in action.

Edison opened a Kinetoscope parlor in New York City in 1894. For a few cents, people could look into the peephole and see a dimly lit "movie," which usually lasted for no more than a minute. The parlor was an instant success, with people entering in droves to see the "peepshows." Kinetoscope parlors soon appeared in other cities in the U.S., as well as in London and Paris.

Despite the popularity of the Kinetoscope, Edison, convinced that moving pictures were just a passing fad, soon turned his attention to other things. In the meantime, several inventors tried their hand at creating motion pictures.

The Lumière Brothers

One of the problems with the Kinetoscope was that only one person at a time could watch through the peephole. The French brothers, Louis and Auguste Lumière, tried to build a device that would show motion pictures to more people.

Working hard to perfect their idea, the Lumière brothers came up with a camera that would both photograph and project films. The camera/projector, called the "Cinématographe," was made of polished brass and mahogany. It stood about five feet tall.

On December 28, 1895, the Lumières made history by projecting a real moving picture on a screen for the first time.

Their films were simple, but they showed the potential for moving pictures. Perhaps their best film was an image of a train arriving at a station. To their fellow Frenchmen the Lumière brothers were heroes.

Edison Takes New Interest

After seeing the Lumières' success, Edison's interest in motion pictures returned. He figured that there was a lot of money to be made

The French brothers, Louis and Auguste Lumière, created a single device called the Cinématographe *that could take pictures **and** project them on a screen.*

from this new industry, and he wanted to be a part of its development. Edison also wanted to beat the Lumières to the American market with his own projection system.

Edison decided the quickest approach was to adapt an existing system, called the Phantoscope, to suit his needs. The Phantoscope was originally developed by two American inventors, Thomas Armat and C. Francis Jenkins. Edison saw the potential of the system, but he made some changes to Armat and Jenkins' basic design and called the device the Projecting Kinescope.

The new projector, later renamed the Edison Vitascope, was introduced to an eager audience at Koster and Bial's Music Hall in New York City on April 23, 1896. Edison presented a film that included scenes from a prize fight, a performance by a dancer, and scenes of waves crashing onto a beach.

Movies Become Popular

The response to Edison's motion pictures was amazing. Within a few years, this new form of entertainment had become a big draw at arcades, theaters, and fairs throughout the world.

In the early days of filmmaking, nearly anything that moved was considered good subject for a film. People gladly paid a few cents to see even the most ordinary events on film. The titles of these early films give an idea of their simple subject matter: *Workers Leaving a Factory*, *Men Playing Cards*, and *Fifty-Ninth Street*.

Although motion pictures were shown in theaters, they weren't very "theatrical." Filmmakers, as well as audiences, were satisfied with just the novelty of seeing moving pictures. Little attention was paid to "telling stories." That all changed with the films of director Edwin S. Porter.

CHAPTER TWO

TELL US A STORY

Edwin Porter's "Robbery"

Edwin S. Porter is known as the first director to use modern film techniques to tell a story. His films— *The Life of An American Fireman* and *The Great Train Robbery*—used techniques that soon changed the industry.

Porter was famous for taking unrelated scenes and making a dramatic film from them. He demonstrated that films could be shot "out of sequence" and then be pieced together for dramatic effect.

In *The Great Train Robbery*, Porter tells the story of a train robbery and the capture of the bandits. Porter created suspense by switching from scenes of the fleeing robbers to scenes of the mob trying to catch them.

Porter is given credit for turning filmmaking into an art form. He created dramatic situations that grabbed the audience's interest.

Nickelodeons

Audiences loved *The Great Train Robbery*. Music halls and vaudeville theaters were packed with eager patrons night after night. The success of this film led to the first motion picture theaters. They were called "nickelodeons" because the price of admission was a nickel.

By 1907 at least 5,000 nickelodeons were operating around the world. In the United States, a new theater opened every day! These theaters weren't very fancy. Often, they were just a screen and chairs piled into an old store or other large building.

Early movies were "silent." Actors "told" the whole story with their movements alone. But silence wasn't necessarily golden! Nickelodeon operators figured out that audiences would pay more money to "hear" a movie as they watched it.

Since the movies themselves couldn't produce sound, piano players were hired to accompany the movies. Their job was to play music that matched the action on the screen.

Movie Studios

The sudden success of nickelodeons caused a shortage of new films. There simply weren't enough to go around.

Pooling their talents, filmmakers soon created the first motion picture "studios." These studios were quickly making hundreds of films each year in the New York area.

In 1911 the Nestor Company built

The Great Train Robbery *was one of the first movies to tell a story. Before that time, audiences were content to see films like* Workers Leaving a Factory.

the first movie studio outside of New York. The location chosen was a small town in Southern California named Hollywood. Within a few years, Hollywood was to become the movie capital of the world—a position it still holds today.

D.W. Griffith

Of the early filmmakers, one man stands out as the "father of motion pictures." D.W. Griffith directed hundreds of short films during his career. He spent these years making better and better movies and developing his unique style. Griffith breathed new life into an industry that was starting to go flat.

Griffith's biggest contribution to filmmaking was the close-up. He would move his cameras closer and closer to the actors to focus the attention of the audience.

D.W. Griffith, at right, is known as the "father of motion pictures." His most famous film is Birth of a Nation.

Until Griffith's time, all action in a scene had been filmed with one camera. The camera usually stayed in the same spot. Instead of moving the camera from scene to scene, the actors and scenery moved!

Griffith used several cameras and many different angles to let the audience see more than one side of the action. To the audience, it was like being in the center of things.

This great director was also a genius when it came to editing films. Like Edwin Porter, Griffith used many short scenes in a row to help tell a more complex story. By switching between shots quickly, Griffith was able to build excitement.

Griffith is famous for his two masterpieces, *The Birth of a Nation* and *Intolerance*. *The Birth of a Nation* was made in 1915 at a cost of more than $110,000. That was an unheard-of budget for a film in those days. The sheer cost of the production drew plenty of attention to the picture even before it reached theaters. Today, it is still considered by some critics to be the greatest motion picture of all time.

Mack Sennett's Keystone Kops

Mack Sennett was one of the many actors employed by D.W. Griffith. Born in Canada, Sennett came to America in 1909 and soon joined up with Griffith.

Sennett learned much of his directing technique from Griffith. When he was still an actor, Sennett would study Griffith's style. At night, he would stand near the studio doors, waiting for Griffith to leave work. He would often join the great director on his walks home. On those walks, Sennett learned a great deal about movie making.

By 1912 Sennett had his own motion picture studio, called Keystone. Sennett's Keystone studio was famous for its wild comedies—many of which featured the Keystone Kops. The Keystone Kops were a bumbling bunch of policemen who always found themselves in a wild chase after somebody or something.

Sennett's movies were circus-like, but they were rooted in reality. The films were set in familiar settings—small towns and villages that people across the world could relate to.

As a director, Sennett became famous for his sense of timing. To produce special effects, he often used slow motion and creative camera angles. Sometimes he even ran the film backwards—which audiences found hilarious.

The comedians in Sennett's films each had an unusual personality or "look" which Sennett played up to grab extra laughs. These comedians included Fatty Arbuckle, Ben Turpin, Charley Chase, and Charlie Chaplin.

The End of Nickelodeons

As movies became more successful, they moved out of nickelodeons and into real theaters. Vaudeville singers, dancers, and comedians were replaced by the "silver screen."

The bumbling Keystone Kops were the subject of many films produced by Mack Sennett. Sennett's films were circus-like, but his directing style was serious.

Audiences poured into theaters by the millions. In exchange for their ticket money, viewers demanded longer and better productions.

Studios scrambled to keep up with the demand. Filmmakers began to adapt popular plays and books into motion pictures. And dozens of famous stage actors headed to Hollywood to seek their fortunes as movie stars.

Mass Production

Studios were having a hard time producing enough movies to keep audiences happy. The shortage of new films was a threat to the entire industry. Then a man named Thomas Ince changed the way movies were made. He introduced production methods that allowed studios to produce more movies at a lower cost.

Mack Sennett's Keystone Studio was a huge complex built in Hollywood's early days. This scene from 1912 shows the movie sets where Sennett's comedies were filmed.

CHAPTER THREE

MOVIES ON A GRAND SCALE

During his first years in the business, Ince directed all of the movies produced by his studio, Thomas Ince Pictures. But he soon realized that he could not keep pace with the demand. He decided to pass some of the work to a group of employees he called "producers." The job of the producer was to supervise the production of a film from start to finish.

Ince planned each movie with the producer before shooting began. He assigned the producer a "budget," which limited the film to a certain number of days of production. At any given time, 10 or more pictures were being produced by the Ince Pictures staff. This was called the "factory system." It was soon used by most studios, all the way up to the 1950's.

The Big Studios

As movie making entered its third decade, a number of studios became leaders in the industry. This group included Metro-Goldwyn-Mayer (MGM), Fox, Columbia, Universal, and Warner Brothers.

As these studios grew, the business end of movies became more complex. The leaders of these studios were businessmen first. To them, art was sometimes less important than money. Profits had to be made! As a result, the 1920's saw few improvements in filmmaking in America. Instead, attention was shifted to building vast chains of theaters and selling American films to foreign countries.

European Influence

During this standstill in America, foreign filmmakers reached their peak of influence. The most lavish films of the 1920's came from Germany. They were produced in huge studios in Berlin. Directors were given almost complete control over the cost of their films—in contrast to the situation in the United States.

German directors used the camera as a means to express emotion, rather than just record it. By using a tight close-up, or unusual angles, the camera became "subjective." In other words, the camera could be placed in such a way that the image it created told more about the scene than the actors or music. For example, a camera shot from below an actor's face or body gave the impression of the character's strength.

Director F.W. Murnau uses such camera effects in *The Last Laugh*. In one touching scene, a doorman has just been demoted to washroom attendant. The shamed doorman is shown drunk. He is collapsed in a chair. The camera is spun around on its base to show the dizziness of the poor man.

The Russian Directors

Russian directors, such as Lev Kuleshov and Sergei Eisenstein, were known for their special editing techniques. One of them was the "montage" technique, in which different images were shown in quick succession. Audiences would emotionally link the images together.

Sergei Eisenstein used the montage technique in his classic film *Potemkin*. The story focused on a mutiny among the crew of a Russian battleship.

In one scene, the viewer sees soldiers firing their rifles. In the next scene, a woman is in agony, holding her stomach. Although it was never actually shown on screen, audiences reacted in horror to the "shooting" of the woman.

The "Talkies"

The first "sound" movies appeared before 1900. Music and other effects were recorded on a phonograph record, which was played as the movie appeared on the screen. But it was a chore for the operator to match the sound to the action. And when the sound didn't fit the action, the effect was almost worse than no sound at all!

For years, little progress was made on talking pictures. Then, in 1927, Bell Laboratories developed an electrical system called the Vitaphone. The Vitaphone passed its first major test in the film *Don Juan*. The Vitaphone was used to add musical effects to the film, but no voices were included in the "soundtrack."

That barrier was broken later in the year with the release of *The Jazz Singer*. This film, starring Al Jolson, was mostly silent, but a few songs and some lines of dialogue were added to the film. It was the first to use voices in a soundtrack.

Al Jolson starred in The Jazz Singer, *which was the first "talking movie." This film changed the motion picture industry forever.*

The *Jazz Singer* marked the end of silent pictures and turned the film industry on end. Once again audiences packed into theaters—to see, and hear, the "talkies." Within two years, movie attendance almost doubled.

Sadly, many actors lost their jobs when the "talkies" took over. Some actors had high-pitched voices or thick foreign accents. Audiences were appalled to hear the voices of some of their favorite stars. Stage actors—with strong voices—were rushed to Hollywood to fill the gap. Fred Astaire, Paul Muni, and Frederic March were among those that found new and lasting careers as film actors.

The New Stars of the 1930's

The 1930's were a golden time for the movies. Audiences flocked to

Oliver Hardy (left) and Stan Laurel (right) were two of the most beloved film stars of all time. Their films are still considered by some to be the funniest ever made.

This film set is typical of the frenzied pace of filmmaking during the 1930's.

see new musicals and comedies. Hollywood produced them as fast as possible to meet the demand. The invention of soundtracks made hits out of films such as *42nd Street, Animal Crackers*, and *The Front Page*.

Actors like Laurel and Hardy, the Marx Brothers, James Cagney, W.C. Fields, Katherine Hepburn, Bob Hope, and Mae West were enormous box-office draws during the 1930's.

The major directors of this period included Frank Capra, John Ford, Alfred Hitchcock, and Victor Fleming. Their work is still considered some of the best filmmaking ever.

Fleming directed the first color epic, *Gone With the Wind,* in 1939. This sweeping story of the Civil War is one of the most popular movies of all time. The movie turned its stars, Clark Gable and Vivian Leigh, into legends.

CHAPTER FOUR

TRYING TO KEEP UP

TV Competes With Movies

The 1950's was a decade of change in the motion picture industry. Television began to pose a major threat to the movies. Though still available only in black and white, TV was becoming very popular.

In some ways, watching TV was just like going to the movies. The shows were entertaining, with lots of action, drama, and comedy. Best of all, once a person bought a television set, watching it was free. Audiences didn't even have to leave home to be entertained!

Filmmakers struggled just to keep up with the "boob tube." Trying to steal some of TV's thunder, Hollywood started a trend toward the "epic" production. Such films had huge budgets and were filmed almost entirely in foreign locations. *Ben Hur* is one example.

Movie makers also made it a special point to show things that still couldn't be seen on TV. Horror films and epic westerns were very popular. They used special effects and scenes that could only be appreciated in color on the big screen.

Another innovation—although it didn't last long—was Cinerama. This process used a wrap-around screen to put audiences right in the middle of the action. Three projectors displayed the image on three sides of the theater. The audience felt like it was a part of what was happening!

The problem with Cinerama was that huge theaters had to be built to handle the system. This was too costly to be practical, and Cinerama soon fell by the wayside.

Movies in 3D (Sort of...)

3D also pumped some life into movies in the 1950's, although it didn't last long. 3D was a process that made things on the screen seem to be real, or three-dimensional—like this book.

To create the effect, a special two-camera filming technique was used. Two projectors, each showing a slightly different image, presented

The Creature From the Black Lagoon *is probably the most famous 3D movie of the 1950's. Viewers were required to wear special glasses to see the unusual 3D effects.*

the film. Audience members had to wear special cardboard glasses that had a different colored lens for each eye. This combination made 3D effects possible.

The 3D effects were supposed to make people feel that they could reach out and touch things on the screen—or that the images on the screen could reach out and touch them. Sometimes the effects worked well, such as in the classic 3D film *Creature From the Black Lagoon*. Most of the time, however, 3D was disappointing. The effects weren't much different from a normal movie.

Scripts for 3D movies were often weak, with plots based on finding new ways to "fling arrows" at the audience. And people didn't like to wear the special glasses, which often caused headaches. As a result, 3D films quickly lost popularity.

The 1960's and 1970's

This period in film history is known as the "reality" years. War was a popular subject, but the films didn't glamorize war as earlier films had. Movies like *M*A*S*H* and *The Deer Hunter* showed the horror of war from the perspective of the people who fought in the Korean and Vietnam wars.

Social issues were also handled differently. Corruption, organized crime, and family breakups were handled with a frank sense of honesty and reality. Films like *The Godfather*, *All the President's Men, Midnight Cowboy*, and *The French Connection* were harder-edged than similar films of previous years. It seemed that no subject was too graphic or controversial to be shown on the screen.

CHAPTER FIVE

A TEAM EFFORT

Making Movies

What we see on the screen is actually the end of the film production effort. Often, years of work have gone into the creation of a film. We are merely witnesses to the final chapter.

Making a motion picture has been compared to going into battle. Literally hundreds of people are involved in the production of a motion picture. From the actors to the person who turns the lights off at the end of a day's shooting, each has a specific job to do. Their skills help the picture move from ideas to the screen.

The Producer

The producer is very important in the process of movie production. This person finds the story to be filmed and gathers the money to make it happen.

Sometimes the producer will arrange the hiring of actors. The producer may even oversee the construction of sets or the design of costumes. Another job is to supervise the work of the director and other important members of the production team.

The Director

The director is the one who actually "makes" the motion picture. This person controls the film crew, making sure that everyone on the set is doing his or her job.

The director must also set up each shot and get the best performances from the actors. In addition, the di-

Alfred Hitchcock is known as one of the great filmmakers. He is best remembered for the high-tension thrillers, Psycho *and* The Birds.

rector—along with a number of assistants—approves the script, sets, costumes, and work schedules.

Besides being a manager, a good director has to have a strong artisic flair. Often it is the director's touch that can make or break a film at the box office.

The Cinematographer

Most people assume that the director is the person behind the camera. While that's true in some cases, the cinematographer operates the camera during most of the filming.

Often the director will look to the cinematographer for advice on what camera or lens to use for a specific scene. The cincmatographer must know how the lighting and other conditions will affect the filming.

In many ways, the cinematographer is a technician as well as an artist.

The Actors

We've all heard of Sylvester Stallone, Jane Fonda, Tom Cruise, and Meryl Streep. They're successful movie stars, and they earn millions of dollars for each film role. But for every Stallone, there are hundreds of actors whose names remain unknown.

Each actor in a film production has a role to play—small or large. Although some roles are obviously more important than others, every actor must do his or her part to help make a movie a success.

A film actor is different from a stage actor in several ways. The stage actor may rehearse for weeks to perform in a three-hour play. The film actor may rehearse for hours to film a few seconds of dialogue. A film actor may also have to perform his or her role "out of sequence." This means that because of scheduling, a performer may have to act out scenes in a different order than they appear in the script. This calls for special talent.

The Designers

There are several types of designers on a movie set. The set designer, sometimes called the art director, oversees the design and construction of the scenery. The set designer must research the time period in which the film is set to make sure that the scenes are accurate. For example, nothing would shock an audience more than to see George Washington wearing a digital watch.

Despite a set director's best efforts, however, these mistakes do happen. Usually, though, they are not so obvious.

The costume designer has many of the same responsibilities. Each costume must reflect the character being portrayed and the time period being filmed. Many costumes take weeks to create!

Makeup and wigs can be as important to the costume director as any piece of clothing. Some science fiction and horror movies rely heav-

The set usually starts with the bare essentials—in this case, little more than walls and a fabric ceiling. When the construction is done, this room will look like the real thing!

ily on special makeup effects. The frightening character of Freddy Krueger, in the *Nightmare on Elm Street* movies, is just one example.

The Editor

One of the most important jobs in movie production is that of film editor. The editor, or "cutter," takes the reels of raw film and puts them together to form the final story.

A film may have thousands of shots, but only a few hundred ever make it into the final production. The editor must use good judgment, an artistic eye, and a strong sense of timing to make everything fit into the time allowed.

The editor must also be able to put scenes together that tell the story without confusing the audience. A choppy, badly-paced movie is often the result of poor editing.

The editor's responsibility hasn't changed much since the early days of filmmaking. The equipment is more sophisticated these days, but the basic skills are the same.

The Composer

Music and sound effects in the movies are almost as important as any words or action on the screen. The wrong sound or music can ruin an otherwise terrific scene.

The composer is hired to create music that fits the mood of the movie. The composer is usually well-trained in all areas of music. He or she may be required to supervise an entire symphony orchestra to get just the right sound for a film.

Today, many films—especially those for teenagers—bypass the composer altogether. Instead, popular music is used as a background for scenes.

Sound effects can also make or break a scene. In *Raiders of the Lost Ark*, for example, much care was put into sound effects, from the hiss of hundreds of snakes to the rumble of a rolling boulder. Each sound is carefully recorded and enhanced to create just the right atmosphere for the scene in which it is used.

A composer may have to conduct a symphony orchestra to make the soundtrack for a movie.

CHAPTER SIX

THE GRAND PRODUCTION

Dollar Signs

After the producer has found a story to use as a basis for a motion picture, the search for financing begins. This process can make or break the movie before filming even begins.

Today, it costs millions of dollars to make a full-length feature film. Some films cost $50 million or more to make! Such "big budget" films are almost always financed by big studios. The amount of money spent on a film depends heavily upon the "name" value of the stars, director, or subject matter.

Many films are now produced by people who have no formal connections to the big studios. These independent producers may look to other sources for financial support.

Once financing is found, a budget will be created. The budget is developed by the studio production department. All of the costs of producing the film—from costumes and sets, to the actors' salaries—are estimated. Once the budget is approved by the studio, the producer and director can begin making the film.

Polishing the Script

Once the financing and budget have been set up, work will begin on the script. A movie script starts out as a simple idea. As the writing process develops, a scriptwriter will "flesh out" the story and make the characters more detailed and complex. The job of the scriptwriter is to create a story that is believable to the audience.

Casting the Film

One of the most important steps in filmmaking is the selection of the cast. This step is called "casting."

Many motion pictures are actually built around a popular star. For example, the *Rambo* movies have been written, directed, and filmed to showcase the talents of Sylvester Stallone. Without Stallone heading the cast, the films probably wouldn't have been as successful as they were. The same is true for *Star Trek* and its sequels. The studio held up production until all members of the original television cast agreed to make the first *Star Trek* movie.

Some producers and directors refuse to hire "name" actors, however. They prefer to use unknowns, who require much less money. Besides, it can be thrilling to showcase new talent on the screen!

It takes a team to put together a film.

On Location

Once the cast is hired, the script polished, and the sets and costumes created, filming will begin. Depending on the script and budget, a movie will either be filmed on location or on a sound stage.

Location shooting means that the entire production will move to a specific location to film certain scenes. This is almost always more expensive than working on a sound stage. For the film *Jaws*, director Steven Speilberg moved the crew to a small town in Massachusetts. They stayed there for several months until filming was completed.

Many of the desert scenes from *Star Wars* and *Raiders of the Lost Ark* were filmed in a real desert. Other movies—like *Ghostbusters*—are filmed in the city in which the story takes place.

Shooting "on location" can cost millions of dollars. People and equipment—sometimes even food and water—must be shipped, trucked, or flown to the film location.

Obviously, location shooting isn't always possible. The battle scenes from *Star Wars* were cooked up in a giant studio by a special effects team. These talented people made it seem like Luke Skywalker and the gang were actually in space!

The Sound Stage

Movies can take months to film. Often, producers and directors find it easier and cheaper to build sets rather than haul a crew on location for weeks or months at a time. Modern directors are able to "fake" the real world so well that audiences never know the difference anyway.

Originally, almost all movies were shot outside. That worked fine if the location was isolated from "outside" noises like airplanes and cars. But the expanding world made finding a truly quiet setting almost

The sound stage is a building where movie magic happens. Nothing compares to the excitement of "lights! cameras! action!" This shows the filming of the 1945 film, Night and Day.

impossible. Sound stages are huge buildings that are built specifically for making motion pictures in a quiet, controlled setting.

The sound stage is generally divided into many smaller stages, or sets. The film crew can film more than one scene at a time on the sound stage. Because of this, a sound stage can look like a spaghetti maze of wircs and cables. Microphones and lights are hung from the ceiling.

Cameras move around the stage on carts or are suspended on giant mechanical arms.

During filming, the pace in the studio can be frantic, to say the least.

Editing the Film

Directors always try to give the editor many different shots of a scene to work with. At the end of a day's shooting, the film is developed.

Some sets—like this western town—are built especially for the movies.

The chariot race from Ben Hur *was one of the most exciting scenes ever filmed.*

These "rushes" are reviewed by the director and the editor. They select the best shots of the day and set them aside for future use. Other shots are discarded—ending up "on the cutting room floor."

When the filming is completed, the editor splices together the rushes into a "rough cut." These shots follow the action in the script. They will be used to create the final film.

Putting It All Together

When the final film has been assembled by the editor, the music and sound effects will be added to the soundtrack. The film and soundtrack are then joined together for the first time.

At this point, the film is shown to "preview" audiences. Cards are handed out to the audience members, who are asked to record their opinion of the film. These cards are reviewed by the director and other members of the production team. If the results are negative, changes may be made to the film before it is released to a wider audience.

When the movie nears completion, the publicity campaign begins.

Newspaper, radio, and television advertisements are prepared. The actors and director may appear on TV or radio programs to promote the film. A "trailer"—like a commerial on TV—is created from the actual film to show in theaters before the main attraction is shown. These short segments are called "previews."

Once the publicity campaign is underway, the film is released to theaters. Most films start out as a limited release, appearing at a few theaters. If the film is a "hit" in these theaters, it is released nationwide.

Not many films last more than a few weeks in theaters. Some, however, will still be shown months—even years—after their initial release. Some of these long-lived movies are called "cult" films. These films may be seen dozens of times by the same people. *The Rocky Horror Picture Show* is one of the better known cult films.

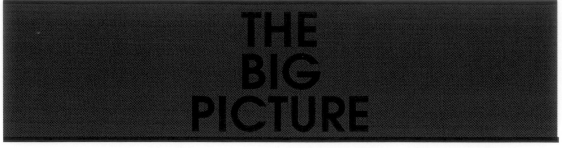

CHAPTER SEVEN

THE BIG PICTURE

Movies Today

In the past ten years, the biggest changes in the movie industry have been in the area of special effects. When people think of special effects, they often think of adventures like *Batman* or science fiction thrillers like *The Fly*. But almost every film uses some type of special effects to make an audience see what isn't really there.

These effects range from mixing cartoons and real actors in *Who Framed Roger Rabbit* to the terrifying makeup of Freddie Krueger in *Nightmare on Elm Street*.

Lots of time and money is spent in making these scenes as realistic and scary as possible. Audiences must love it, because they keep coming back for more!

Movies on Video

Nearly half of all American homes have a video cassette recorder. These machines allow people to record movies and shows off TV, or rent movies from a store to watch at home.

A big reason for the popularity of VCR's is the viewing freedom that they offer. While a local theater may only show a few films on any given day, a person can walk into a video rental store and choose from thousands of films that once appeared in theaters. And a movie on videocasette usually rents for less than the cost of a single theater ticket. An entire family can see a movie in their home for just a few dollars.

Some movies are never shown in theaters. They are "made for video." These films are usually made on a

An artist puts the finishing touches on a drawing. This drawing, and thousands of others, will be photographed as part of an animated sequence.

low budget and appeal to a limited audience. More and more of these films are being made today.

The Future

The movie industry has faced many challenges over the years, especially from TV. And now the battle lines are drawn once more—between the silver screen and the boob tube.

As it was in the 1950's, TV is the biggest competitor to movies. Every year, new channels spring up on cable TV. Videocassettes hit stores by the truckload. And 3D on TV is a very real possibility. Each new feat helps TV compete for the same audience.

Still, the past few years have been the best ever at the box office. The technical wizardry displayed in films like *E.T.* and *Captain EO* draws people into theaters. And there's a certain magic about the big silver screen that makes comedies funnier and dramas more moving.

Besides, there's nothing like sitting inside a dark theater with your friends—and a big tub of buttered popcorn!

Video cassette recorders allow people to enjoy movies in their own homes. Nearly half of all U.S. households have a VCR!

Charie Chaplin's character in The Gold Rush *is glum, but he and countless others have brought joy to generations of moviegoers. That's something to smile about!*

GLOSSARY

budget—a plan, usually put together by a studio, to show filmmakers how much money they may spend on a film.

camera angles—the direction the camera is facing; can give a certain point of view to a shot.

celluloid—a plastic material to which film is applied; used in spools or reels to allow film to quickly be moved through a camera.

develop—to apply chemicals to exposed film causing an image to appear.

dialogue—the spoken words in a movie.

epic—a movie that tells a larger-than-life story about a legendary hero or event.

intolerance—not allowing actions or thoughts that are different than one's own.

microphone—a device that picks up sound and turns it into electrical signals which can then be amplified and recorded.

phonograph—record player; a device that picks up sounds from a record.

projector—a device used to enlarge and display an image.

rushes—developed film from a day's shooting; used to review scenes.

sequence—the order in which something is done; some movies are filmed "out of sequence" to save time or money.

shutter—a device behind a camera lens; opens to let in light to expose film.

slow motion—movement that is slowed to make quick action more easily observed.

sound track—the music, sound effects, and words that go with a movie.

splice—joining two film sections together to create a single section.

story line—the plot of a movie.

studio—a building or place where movies are filmed; movie companies are sometimes called studios, too.

subjective—a point of view; filmmakers use special camera angles or other techniques to make the audience feel a certain way about a character.

technician—someone with special talents or skills who is responsible for a particular job.

three-dimensional, or 3D—an effect that makes objects on the screen seem to have a realistic shape or texture.

trailer—an advertisement for a movie; it is usually shown in theaters as a "preview" of a coming attraction.

vaudeville—a stage performance style of the early part of the 1900's; included singers, dancers, and comics.

INDEX

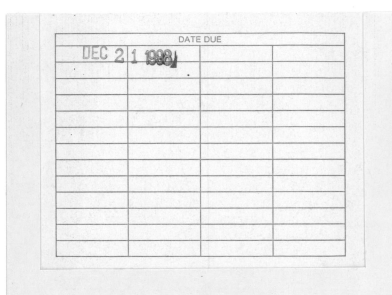